POPULAR SONGS

HAL LEONARD STUDENT PIANO LIBRARY

INTERMEDIATE PIANO SOLOS

Movie Blockbusters

Arranged by Mona Rejino

T0081818

ISBN 978-1-4950-9318-0

HAL•LEONARD®

7777 W. BLUEMOUND RD. P.O. BOX 13819 MILWAUKEE, WI 53213

For all works contained herein:
Unauthorized copying, arranging, adapting, recording, Internet posting, public performance,
or other distribution of the printed music in this publication is an infringement of copyright.
Infringers are liable under the law.

Visit Hal Leonard Online at
www.halleonard.com

From the Arranger

It's hard to imagine viewing your favorite movies without the musical score that sets the mood and enriches the experience. We often leave the cinema with that beautiful melody, dramatic theme, or catchy tune playing in our head for days afterwards.

This collection includes some of the most popular movie theme songs in recent years. My hope is that you will enjoy bringing these arrangements to life and making them your own.

Mona Rejino

An accomplished pianist, composer, arranger, and teacher, **Mona Rejino** maintains an independent piano studio in Carrollton, Texas. She also teaches privately at the Hockaday School and is a frequent adjudicator in the Dallas area. A member of *Who's Who of American Women*, Mona received her music degrees from West Texas State University and the University of North Texas. She and her husband, Richard, often present programs on a variety of topics for music teacher associations throughout Texas as well as nationally.

CONTENTS

Can't Stop the Feeling

from TROLLS

Words and Music by Justin Timberlake,
Max Martin and Shellback
Arranged by Mona Rejino

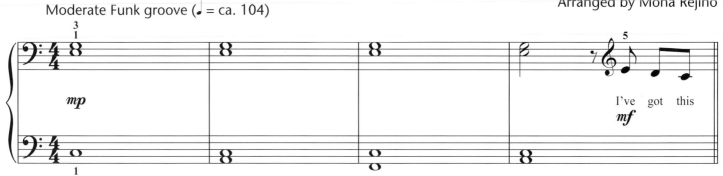

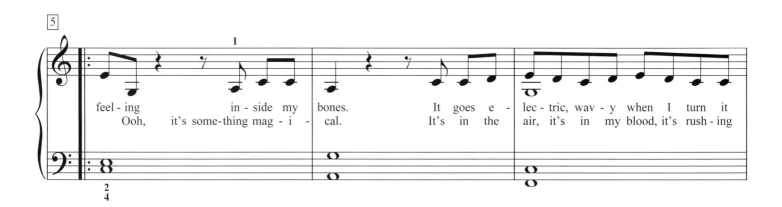

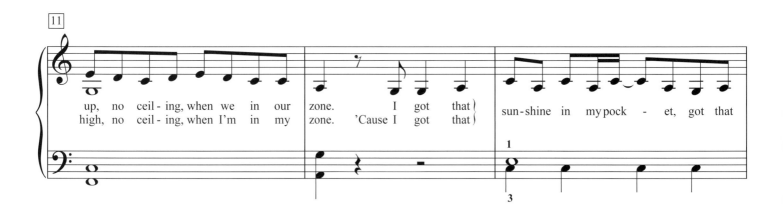

Copyright © 2016 by Universal Music - Z Tunes LLC, Tennman Tunes, DWA Songs and MXM
This arrangement Copyright © 2018 by Universal Music - Z Tunes LLC, Tennman Tunes, DWA Songs and MXM
All Rights for Tennman Tunes Administered by Universal Music - Z Tunes LLC
All Rights for DWA Songs Administered by Almo Music Corp.
All Rights for MXM Administered Worldwide by Kobalt Songs Music Publishing
International Copyright Secured   All Rights Reserved

good soul in my feet. I feel that hot blood in my bod — y when it drops, ooh. — I can't

take my eyes up off — it, mov-ing so phe-nom - e-nal-ly. Room on lock, the way we rock — it, so don't

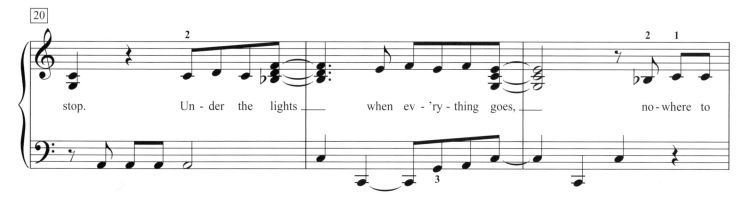

stop. Un - der the lights — when ev - 'ry-thing goes, — no-where to

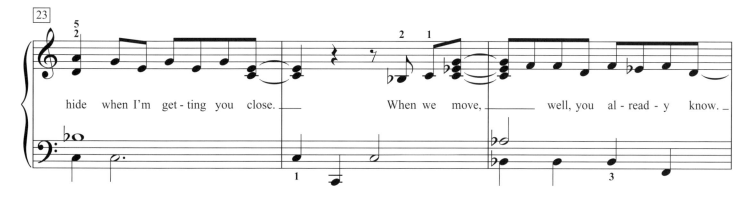

hide when I'm get - ting you close. — When we move, — well, you al - read - y know. —

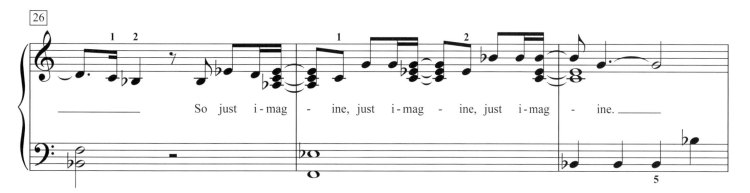

— So just i-mag - ine, just i-mag - ine, just i-mag - ine. —

Noth-ing I can see but you when you dance, dance, dance. A feel-ing good, good creep-ing up on you, so just

dance, dance, dance. Come on! All those things I should-n't do, but you dance, dance, dance. And ain't_

_ no-bod-y leav-ing soon, so keep danc - ing. I can't stop the feel - ing, so just

dance, dance, dance. I can't stop the feel - ing. _ So just dance, dance, dance. Come on!

dance, dance, dance. I can't stop the feel - ing. So just dance, dance, dance. I can't stop the feel -

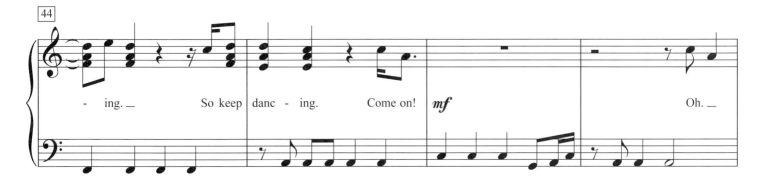

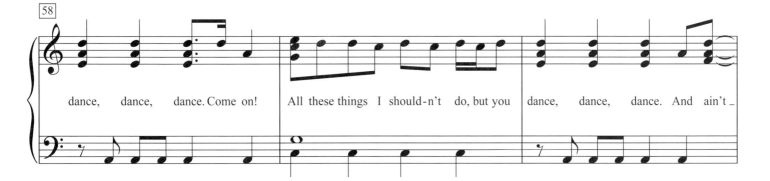

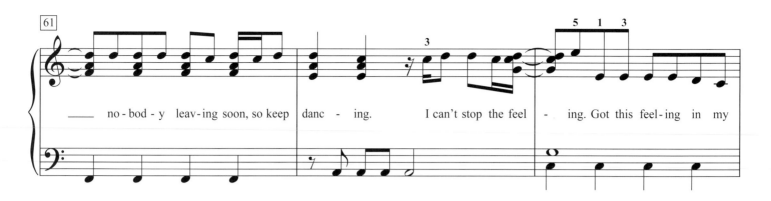

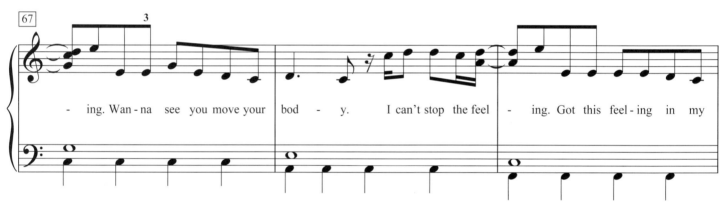

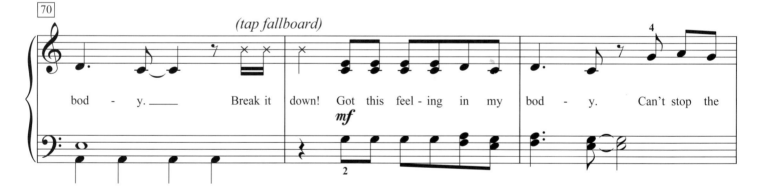

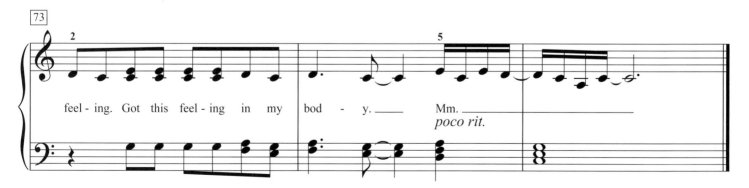

Finding Dory

(Main Title)

from FINDING DORY

Music by Thomas Newman
Arranged by Mona Rejino

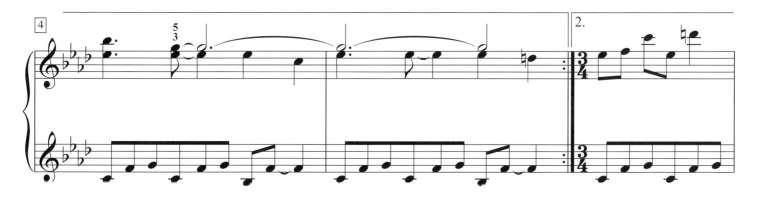

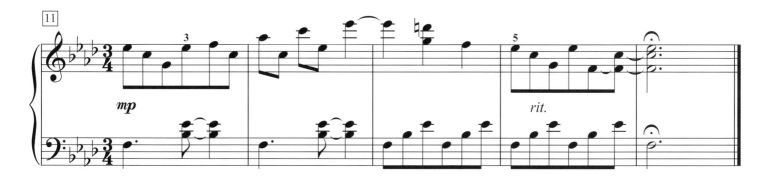

© 2016 Wonderland Music Company, Inc. and Pixar Music
All Rights Reserved. Used by Permission.

How Far I'll Go

from MOANA

Music and Lyrics by
Lin-Manuel Miranda
Arranged by Mona Rejino

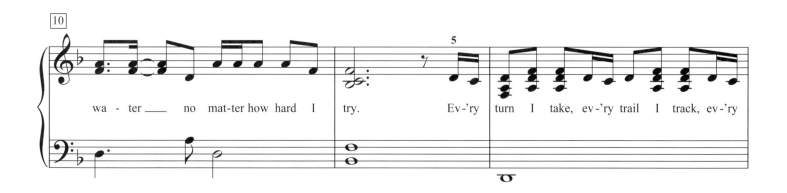

© 2016 Walt Disney Music Company
All Rights Reserved. Used by Permission.

path I make, ev -'ry road leads back to the place I know where I can - not go, where I

long __ to be. See the line where the sky meets the sea, it calls __ me, and no one

knows _____ how far it goes. _____ If the wind in my sail on the sea stays be - hind _

__ me, one day I'll know. _____ If I go, there's just no tell-ing how far I'll

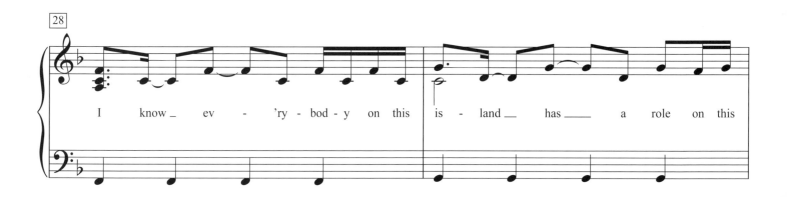

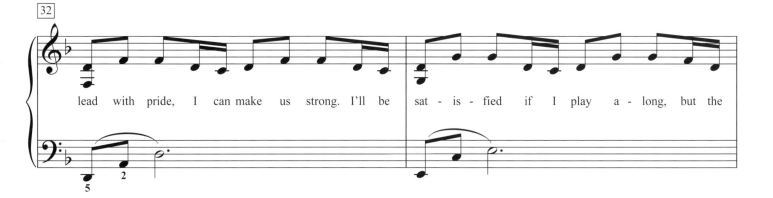

lead with pride, I can make us strong. I'll be sat - is - fied if I play a - long, but the

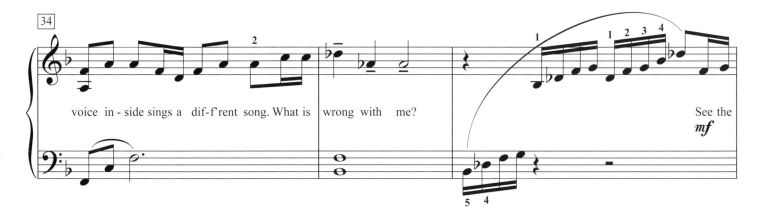

voice in - side sings a dif-f'rent song. What is wrong with me? See the

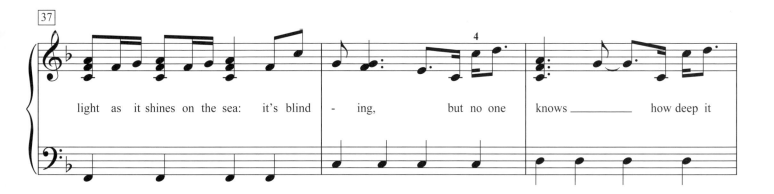

light as it shines on the sea: it's blind - ing, but no one knows _____ how deep it

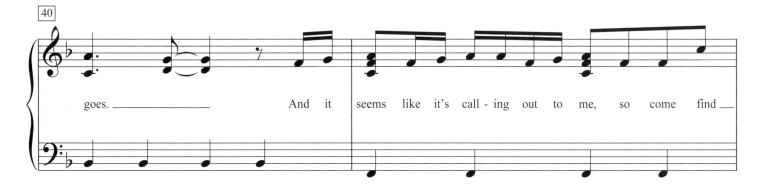

goes. _____ And it seems like it's call - ing out to me, so come find _

_____ me   and let me   know. _____   What's be - yond that line? Will I cross that line?   The

line where the sky meets the sea,   it   calls ___ me,   and no one   knows _____ how far it

goes. _____   If the wind in my sail on the sea stays be - hind ___ me,   one day I'll

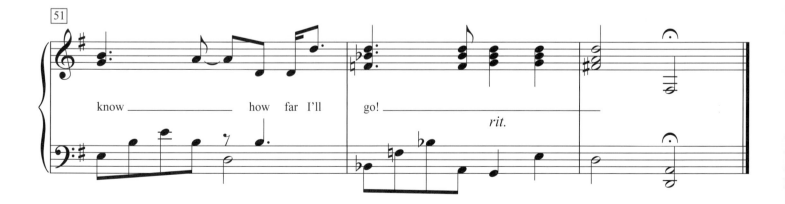

know _____ how far I'll   go! _____   _rit._

The Imperial Suite

from ROGUE ONE: A STAR WARS STORY

Music by Michael Giacchino
Arranged by Mona Rejino

Moderately, in 2, steadily (♩ = ca. 80)

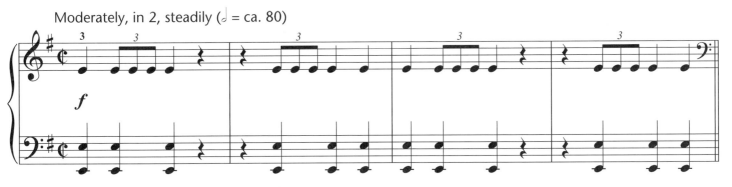

© 2016 Wampa Tauntaun Music
All Rights Reserved. Used by Permission.

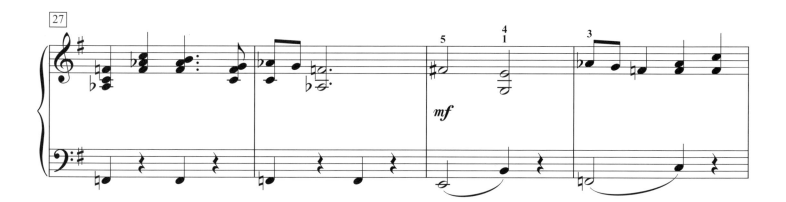

Just Like Fire

from ALICE THROUGH THE LOOKING GLASS (WDP)

Words and Music by Alecia Moore,
Max Martin, Shellback and Oscar Holter
Arranged by Mona Rejino

© 2016 Walt Disney Music Company, Wonderland Music Company, Inc., EMI Blackwood Music Inc., Pink Inside Publishing,
MXM, Lionheart Music, Wolf Cousins and Warner/Chappell Music Scandinavia AB
All Rights for EMI Blackwood Music Inc. and Pink Inside Publishing Administered by Sony/ATV Music Publishing LLC, 424 Church Street, Suite 1200, Nashville, TN 37219
All Rights for MXM Administered Worldwide by Kobalt Songs Music Publishing
All Rights for Lionheart Music in the United States and Canada Administered by Universal - PolyGram International Tunes, Inc.
All Rights for Wolf Cousins and Warner/Chappell Music Scandinavia AB Administered by WB Music Corp.
All Rights Reserved.   Used by Permission.

E - ven when I give it all a - way, I want it all, ____ mm. ____ We came here to
We don't have to wor - ry 'bout a thing, a - bout a thing, ____ no. ____

mp

run it, run it, run it. We came here to run it, run it, run it. Just like

mf

fi - re, burn - ing up the way, if I can light the world up for just one day, watch this

mad - ness, col - or - ful cha - rade. No one can be just like me an - y - way. Just like

mag - ic, I'll be fly - ing free. I'm a dis - ap - pear when they come for me. I kick that

ceil - ing; what you gon - na say? No one can be just like me an - y - way. Just like

fi - re. _mp_ And fi - re. _mf_ Run it,

run it. We came here to run it, run it, run it.

Rap: *(See additional lyrics)*
_mp_

Mm, what's a girl to do? ___ Hey, ___ what's a girl to do? ___ Ah, ___
_mf_

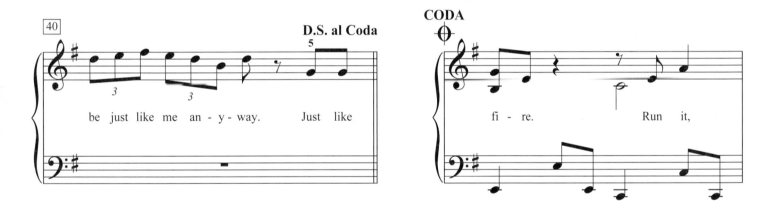

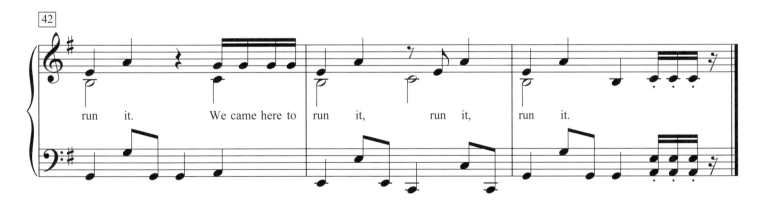

Additional Lyrics

Rap: So look, I came here to run it, just 'cause nobody's done it.
Y'all don't think I could run it, but look, I've been here, I've done it.
Impossible? Please! Watch, I do it with ease.
You just gotta believe. Come on, come on with me.

Mia & Sebastian's Theme

from LA LA LAND

Music by Justin Hurwitz
Arranged by Mona Rejino

© 2016 B Lion Music (BMI)/Warner-Tamerlane Publishing Corp. (BMI) administered by Warner-Tamerlane Publishing Corp. (BMI)
This arrangement © 2018 B Lion Music (BMI)/Warner-Tamerlane Publishing Corp. (BMI) administered by Warner-Tamerlane Publishing Corp. (BMI)
All Rights Reserved   Used by Permission

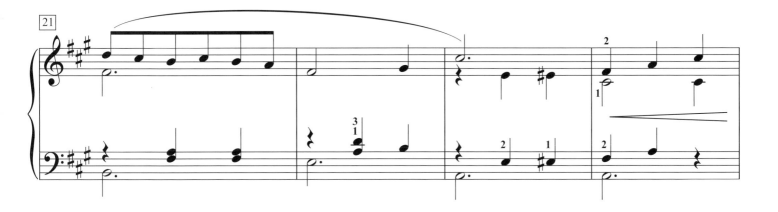

As fast as possible, freely

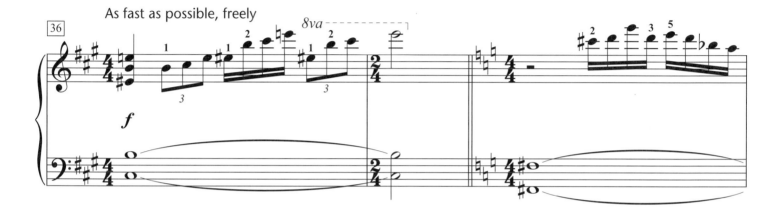

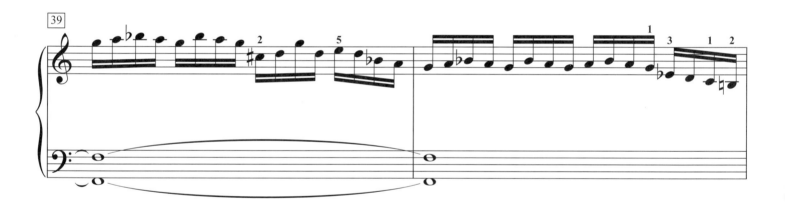

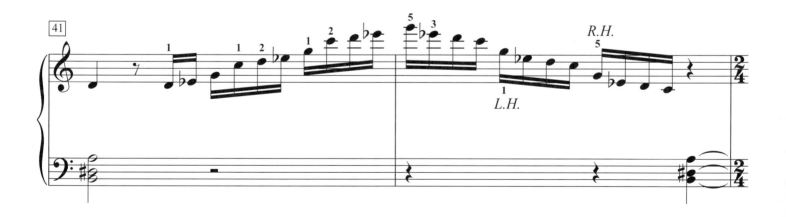

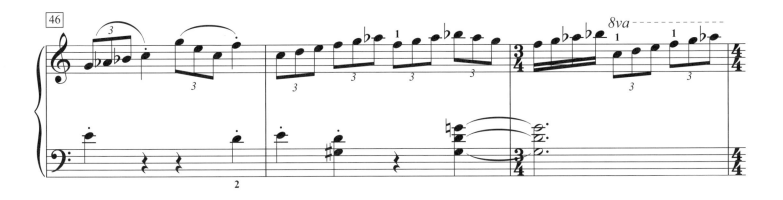

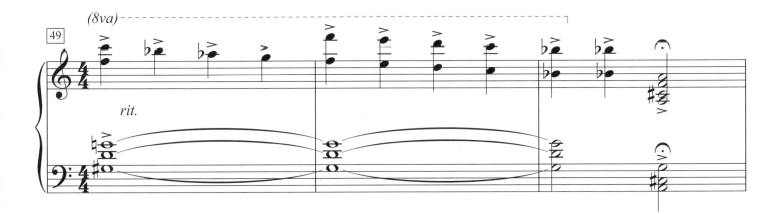

Rey's Theme

from STAR WARS: THE FORCE AWAKENS

Music by John Williams
Arranged by Mona Rejino

Moderately, steadily (♩ = ca. 100)

© 2015 Utapau Music
All Rights Reserved. Used by Permission.

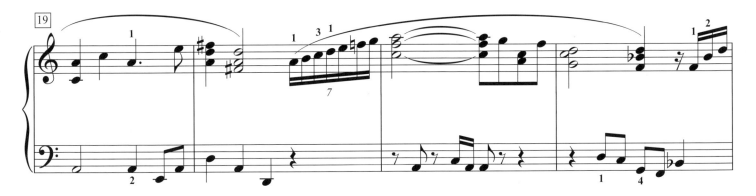

Set It All Free

from SING

Words and Music by
Dave Bassett

Driving Rock (♩ = ca. 132)

I fol-lowed my heart in-to the fi-re, got burned, got bro-ken down

by de-si-re. I tried, I tried,_ but the smoke in my eyes_ left me

blur-ry, blur-ry and blind._ I picked all the piec-es up
I was a girl caught un-

_ off the ground._ I burned all my fin-gers, but that's_ gone now._ Got the
-der your thumb,_ but my star's gon-na shine_ bright-er than your sun._ And I will

Copyright © 2016 Know Your Writes and Universal Pictures Music
This arrangement Copyright © 2018 Know Your Writes and Universal Pictures Music
All Rights for Know Your Writes Administered by Kobalt Songs Music Publishing
All Rights for Universal Pictures Music Controlled and Administered by Universal Music Corp.
All Rights Reserved   Used by Permission

glue in my hands, _ I'm stick - ing to the plan,
reach _ so high, _____ shoot so _ far, _ gon - na

stick-ing to the plan that says _
hit, _ gon - na hit, hit _

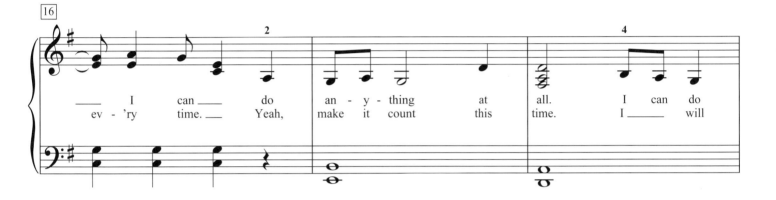

_____ I can _____ do an - y - thing at all. I can do
ev - 'ry time. _ Yeah, make it count this time. I _____ will

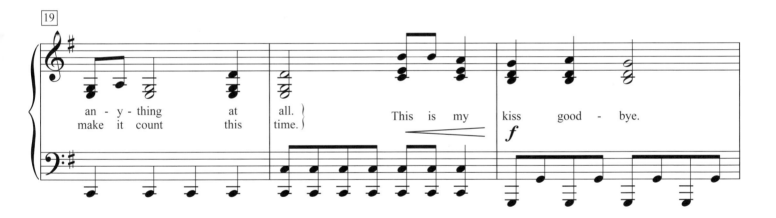

an - y - thing at all. _
make it count this time. _

This is my kiss good - bye.

𝆑

You can stand _ a - lone and watch me fly, _ 'cause noth-ing's keep-ing me

down, gon - na let it all out. Come on and say it right now, right now, right

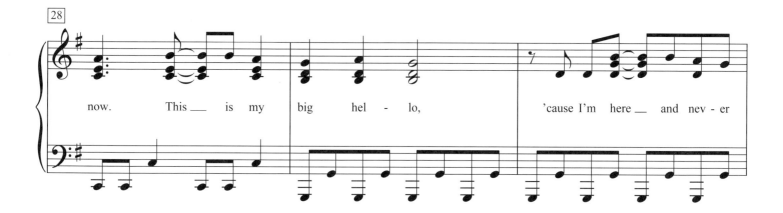

now. This __ is my big hel - lo, 'cause I'm here __ and nev - er

let - ting go. __ I can fi - nal - ly see it's not __ just a

To Coda ⊕

dream when you set it all free, all free, all free. You set it all

This is my kiss good-bye. You can stand _ a-lone and watch me fly, _

'cause noth-ing's keep-ing me down, gon-na let it all out. Come on and say it right

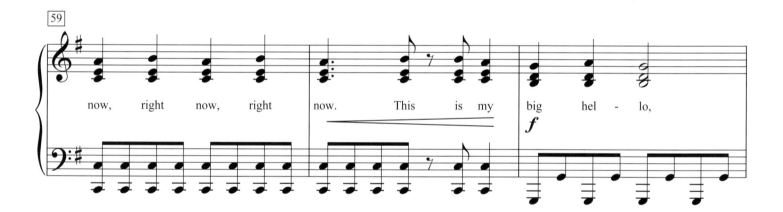

now, right now, right now. This is my big hel-lo,

'cause I'm here _ and nev-er let-ting go. _ I can fi-nal-ly

see it's not just a dream when you set it all free, all free, all

free. You set it all free. You set it all

free. You set it all free.

You set it all free. You set it all free.

POPULAR SONGS
HAL LEONARD STUDENT PIANO LIBRARY

The **Hal Leonard Student Piano Library** has great songs, and you will find all your favorites here: Disney classics, Broadway and movie favorites, and today's top hits. These graded collections are skillfully and imaginatively arranged for students and pianists at every level, from elementary solos with teacher accompaniments to sophisticated piano solos for the advancing pianist.

Adele
arr. Mona Rejino
00159590 Correlates with HLSPL Level 5..........$12.99

The Beatles
arr. Eugénie Rocherolle
00296649 Correlates with HLSPL Level 5..........$10.99

Irving Berlin Piano Duos
arr. Don Heitler and Jim Lyke
00296838 Correlates with HLSPL Level 5..........$14.99

Broadway Hits
arr. Carol Klose
00296650 Correlates with HLSPL Levels 4/5........$8.99

Chart Hits
arr. Mona Rejino
00296710 Correlates with HLSPL Level 5.............$8.99

Christmas Cheer
arr. Phillip Keveren
00296616 Correlates with HLSPL Level 4.............$6.95

Classic Christmas Favorites
arr. Jennifer & Mike Watts
00129582 Correlates with HLSPL Level 5.............$9.99

Christmas Time Is Here
arr. Eugénie Rocherolle
00296614 Correlates with HLSPL Level 5.............$8.99

Classic Joplin Rags
arr. Fred Kern
00296743 Correlates with HLSPL Level 5.............$9.99

**Classical Pop –
Lady Gaga Fugue & Other Pop Hits**
arr. Giovanni Dettori
00296921 Correlates with HLSPL Level 5..........$12.99

Contemporary Movie Hits
arr. by Carol Klose, Jennifer Linn and Wendy Stevens
00296780 Correlates with HLSPL Level 5.............$8.99

Contemporary Pop Hits
arr. Wendy Stevens
00296836 Correlates with HLSPL Level 3.............$8.99

Country Favorites
arr. Mona Rejino
00296861 Correlates with HLSPL Level 5.............$9.99

Current Hits
arr. Mona Rejino
00296768 Correlates with HLSPL Level 5.............$8.99

Disney Favorites
arr. Phillip Keveren
00296647 Correlates with HLSPL Levels 3/4........$9.99

Disney Film Favorites
arr. Mona Rejino
00296809 Correlates with HLSPL Level 5..........$10.99

Easy Christmas Duets
arr. Mona Rejino and Phillip Keveren
00237139 Correlates with HLSPL Level 3/4 ....$9.99

Four Hands on Broadway
arr. Fred Kern
00146177 Correlates with HLSPL Level 5..........$12.99

Jazz Hits for Piano Duet
arr. Jeremy Siskind
00143248 Correlates with HLSPL Level 5 ....$10.99

Elton John
arr. Carol Klose
00296721 Correlates with HLSPL Level 5.............$8.99

Joplin Ragtime Duets
arr. Fred Kern
00296771 Correlates with HLSPL Level 5.............$8.99

Jerome Kern Classics
arr. Eugénie Rocherolle
00296577 Correlates with HLSPL Level 5..........$12.99

Pop Hits for Piano Duet
arr. Jeremy Siskind
00224734 Correlates with HLSPL Level 5..........$10.99

Sing to the King
arr. Phillip Keveren
00296808 Correlates with HLSPL Level 5.............$8.99

Spooky Halloween Tunes
arr. Fred Kern
00121550 Correlates with HLSPL Levels 3/4........$9.99

Today's Hits
arr. Mona Rejino
00296646 Correlates with HLSPL Level 5.............$7.99

Top Hits
arr. Jennifer and Mike Watts
00296894 Correlates with HLSPL Level 5..........$10.99

Top Piano Ballads
arr. Jennifer Watts
00197926 Correlates with HLSPL Level 5..........$10.99

You Raise Me Up
arr. Deborah Brady
00296576 Correlates with HLSPL Levels 2/3........$7.95

7777 W. BLUEMOUND RD. P.O. BOX 13819 MILWAUKEE, WI 53213

Visit our website at **www.halleonard.com**

Prices, contents and availability subject to change without notice. Prices may vary outside the U.S.

COMPOSER SHOWCASE

HAL LEONARD STUDENT PIANO LIBRARY

This series showcases great original piano music from our **Hal Leonard Student Piano Library** family of composers. Carefully graded for easy selection, each book contains gems that are certain to become tomorrow's classics!

BILL BOYD

JAZZ BITS (AND PIECES)
Early Intermediate Level
00290312 11 Solos.............................$7.99

JAZZ DELIGHTS
Intermediate Level
00240435 11 Solos.............................$7.99

JAZZ FEST
Intermediate Level
00240436 10 Solos.............................$8.99

JAZZ PRELIMS
Early Elementary Level
00290032 12 Solos.............................$7.99

JAZZ SKETCHES
Intermediate Level
00220001 8 Solos...............................$8.99

JAZZ STARTERS
Elementary Level
00290425 10 Solos.............................$7.99

JAZZ STARTERS II
Late Elementary Level
00290434 11 Solos.............................$7.99

JAZZ STARTERS III
Late Elementary Level
00290465 12 Solos.............................$8.99

THINK JAZZ!
Early Intermediate Level
00290417 Method Book..................$12.99

TONY CARAMIA

JAZZ MOODS
Intermediate Level
00296728 8 Solos...............................$6.95

SUITE DREAMS
Intermediate Level
00296775 4 Solos...............................$6.99

SONDRA CLARK

THREE ODD METERS
Intermediate Level
00296472 3 Duets..............................$6.95

MATTHEW EDWARDS

CONCERTO FOR YOUNG PIANISTS
FOR 2 PIANOS, FOUR HANDS
Intermediate Level Book/CD
00296356 3 Movements $19.99

CONCERTO NO. 2 IN G MAJOR
FOR 2 PIANOS, 4 HANDS
Intermediate Level Book/CD
00296670 3 Movements..................$17.99

PHILLIP KEVEREN

MOUSE ON A MIRROR
Late Elementary Level
00296361 5 Solos...............................$7.99

MUSICAL MOODS
Elementary/Late Elementary Level
00296714 7 Solos...............................$5.95

SHIFTY-EYED BLUES
Late Elementary Level
00296374 5 Solos...............................$7.99

CAROL KLOSE

THE BEST OF CAROL KLOSE
Early Intermediate to Late Intermediate Level
00146151 15 Solos...........................$12.99

CORAL REEF SUITE
Late Elementary Level
00296354 7 Solos...............................$6.99

DESERT SUITE
Intermediate Level
00296667 6 Solos...............................$7.99

FANCIFUL WALTZES
Early Intermediate Level
00296473 5 Solos...............................$7.95

GARDEN TREASURES
Late Intermediate Level
00296787 5 Solos...............................$7.99

ROMANTIC EXPRESSIONS
Intermediate/Late Intermediate Level
00296923 5 Solos...............................$8.99

WATERCOLOR MINIATURES
Early Intermediate Level
00296848 7 Solos...............................$7.99

JENNIFER LINN

AMERICAN IMPRESSIONS
Intermediate Level
00296471 6 Solos...............................$8.99

ANIMALS HAVE FEELINGS TOO
Early Elementary/Elementary Level
00147789 8 Solos...............................$7.99

CHRISTMAS IMPRESSIONS
Intermediate Level
00296706 8 Solos...............................$8.99

JUST PINK
Elementary Level
00296722 9 Solos...............................$8.99

LES PETITES IMAGES
Late Elementary Level
00296664 7 Solos...............................$8.99

LES PETITES IMPRESSIONS
Intermediate Level
00296355 6 Solos...............................$7.99

REFLECTIONS
Late Intermediate Level
00296843 5 Solos...............................$7.99

TALES OF MYSTERY
Intermediate Level
00296769 6 Solos...............................$8.99

LYNDA LYBECK-ROBINSON

ALASKA SKETCHES
Early Intermediate Level
00119637 8 Solos...............................$7.99

AN AWESOME ADVENTURE
Late Elementary Level
00137563..$7.99

FOR THE BIRDS
Early Intermediate/Intermediate Level
00237078 ....$8.99

MONA REJINO

CIRCUS SUITE
Late Elementary Level
00296665 5 Solos...............................$6.99

COLOR WHEEL
Early Intermediate Level
00201951 6 Solos...............................$8.99

JUST FOR KIDS
Elementary Level
00296840 8 Solos...............................$7.99

MERRY CHRISTMAS MEDLEYS
Intermediate Level
00296799 5 Solos...............................$8.99

MINIATURES IN STYLE
Intermediate Level
00148088 6 Solos...............................$8.99

PORTRAITS IN STYLE
Early Intermediate Level
00296507 6 Solos...............................$8.99

EUGÉNIE ROCHEROLLE

CELEBRATION SUITE
ORIGINAL DUETS FOR ONE PIANO, FOUR HANDS
Intermediate Level
00152724 3 Duets..............................$8.99

ENCANTOS ESPAÑOLES
(SPANISH DELIGHTS)
Intermediate Level
00125451 6 Solos...............................$8.99

JAMBALAYA
FOR 2 PIANOS, 8 HANDS
Intermediate Level
00296654 Piano Ensemble..............$10.99

JAMBALAYA
FOR 2 PIANOS, 4 HANDS
Intermediate Level
00296725 Piano Duo (2 Pianos) $7.95

LITTLE BLUES CONCERTO
FOR 2 PIANOS, 4 HANDS
Early Intermediate Level
00142801..$12.99

TOUR FOR TWO
Late Elementary Level
00296832 6 Duets..............................$7.99

TREASURES
Late Elementary/Early Intermediate Level
00296924 7 Solos...............................$8.99

CHRISTOS TSITSAROS

DANCES FROM AROUND THE WORLD
Early Intermediate Level
00296688 7 Solos...............................$6.95

LYRIC BALLADS
Intermediate/Late Intermediate Level
00102404 6 Solos...............................$8.99

POETIC MOMENTS
Intermediate Level
00296403 8 Solos...............................$8.99

SONATINA HUMORESQUE
Late Intermediate Level
00296772 3 Movements....................$6.99

SONGS WITHOUT WORDS
Intermediate Level
00296506 9 Solos...............................$7.95

THREE PRELUDES
Early Advanced Level
00130747 ....$8.99

THROUGHOUT THE YEAR
Late Elementary Level
00296723 12 Duets............................$6.95

ADDITIONAL COLLECTIONS

AMERICAN PORTRAITS
by Wendy Stevens
Intermediate Level
00296817 6 Solos...............................$7.99

AT THE LAKE
by Elvina Pearce
Elementary/Late Elementary Level
00131642 10 Solos and Duets...........$7.99

COUNTY RAGTIME FESTIVAL
by Fred Kern
Intermediate Level
00296882 7 Rags................................$7.99

LITTLE JAZZERS
by Jennifer Watts
Elementary/Late Elementary Level
00154573 Solos...................................8.99

MYTHS AND MONSTERS
by Jeremy Siskind
Late Elementary/Early Intermediate Level
00148148 9 Solos...............................$7.99

PLAY THE BLUES!
by Luann Carman (Method Book)
Early Intermediate Level
00296357 10 Solos.............................$9.99

Prices, contents, and availability subject
to change without notice.

HAL•LEONARD®

www.halleonard.com